DO YOU REALLY WANT TO MEET DIPLODOCUS?

BY ANNETTE BAY PIMENTEL • ILLUSTRATED BY DANIELE FABBRI

AMICUS ILLUSTRATED and AMICUS INK
are published by Amicus
P.O. Box 1329, Mankato, MN 56002
www.amicuspublishing.us

EDITOR: Alissa Thielges
SERIES DESIGNER: Kathleen Petelinsek
BOOK DESIGNER: Veronica Scott

LIBRARY OF CONGRESS CATALOGING-IN-PUBLICATION DATA
Names: Pimentel, Annette Bay, author. | Fabbri, Daniele,
    1978- illustrator.
Title: Do you really want to meet diplodocus? / by Annette
    Bay Pimentel ;   illustrated by Daniele Fabbri.
Description: Mankato, Minnesota : Amicus, [2020] | Series:
    Do you really want to meet a dinosaur? | Audience: K
    to Grade 3. | Includes bibliographical references.
Identifiers: LCCN 2018029360 (print) | LCCN 2018035699
    (ebook) | ISBN 9781681517889 (pdf) | ISBN 9781681517063
    (library binding) | ISBN 9781681524924 (paperback)
Subjects: LCSH: Diplodocus--Juvenile literature. |
    Dinosaurs--Juvenile literature.
Classification: LCC QE862.S3 (ebook) | LCC QE862.S3 P558
    2020 (print) | DDC 567.913--dc23
LC record available at https://lccn.loc.gov/2018029360

Printed in the United States of America
HC 10 9 8 7 6 5 4 3 2 1
PB 10 9 8 7 6 5 4 3 2 1

ABOUT THE AUTHOR
Annette Bay Pimentel lives in Moscow, Idaho with her family.
She doesn't have a time machine, so she researches the
past at the library. She writes about what happened a
long time ago in nonfiction picture books like *Mountain Chef*
(2016, Charlesbridge). You can visit her online at
www.annettebaypimentel.com.

ABOUT THE ILLUSTRATOR
Daniele Fabbri was born in Ravenna, Italy, in 1978. He
graduated from Istituto Europeo di Design in Milan,
Italy, and started his career as a cartoon animator,
storyboarder, and background designer for animated
series. He has worked as a freelance illustrator since 2003,
collaborating with advertising agencies and international
publishers, including many books for Amicus.

You love giraffes. Did you know Diplodocus was a dinosaur and had an even longer neck? It is extinct, so you won't find it in a zoo. Do you really want to meet a Diplodocus?

Find a time machine and you can meet that giant plant eater! Go back 150 million years to the Jurassic Period. Head for Wyoming—that's where many Diplodocus fossils have been found.

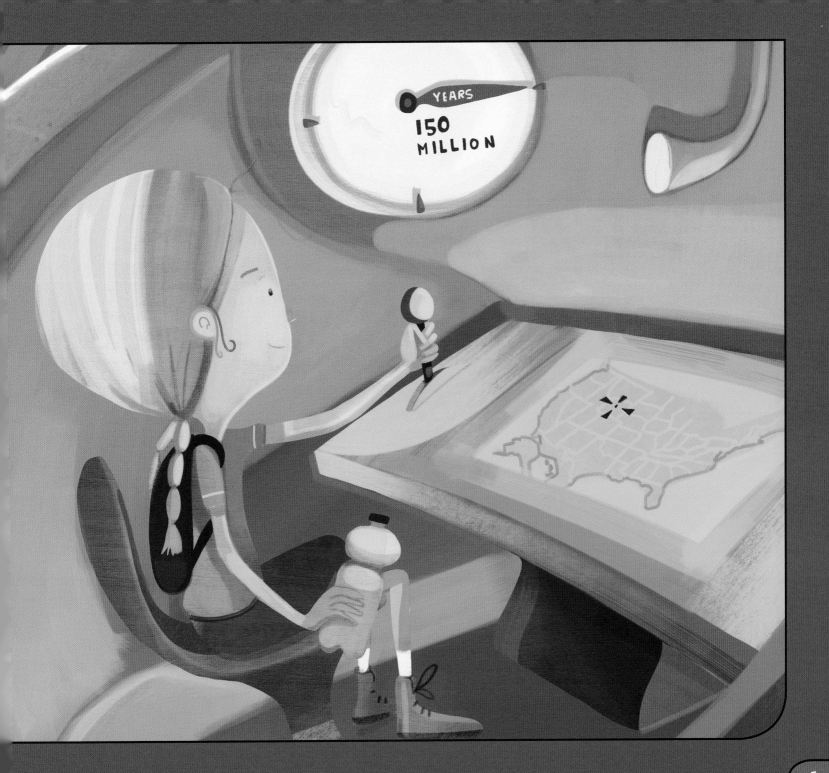

You've arrived in the dry season. Make sure to take your water with you. It's hot here with very little rainfall.

Head toward that thicket. Diplodocus herds usually graze there, near the river.

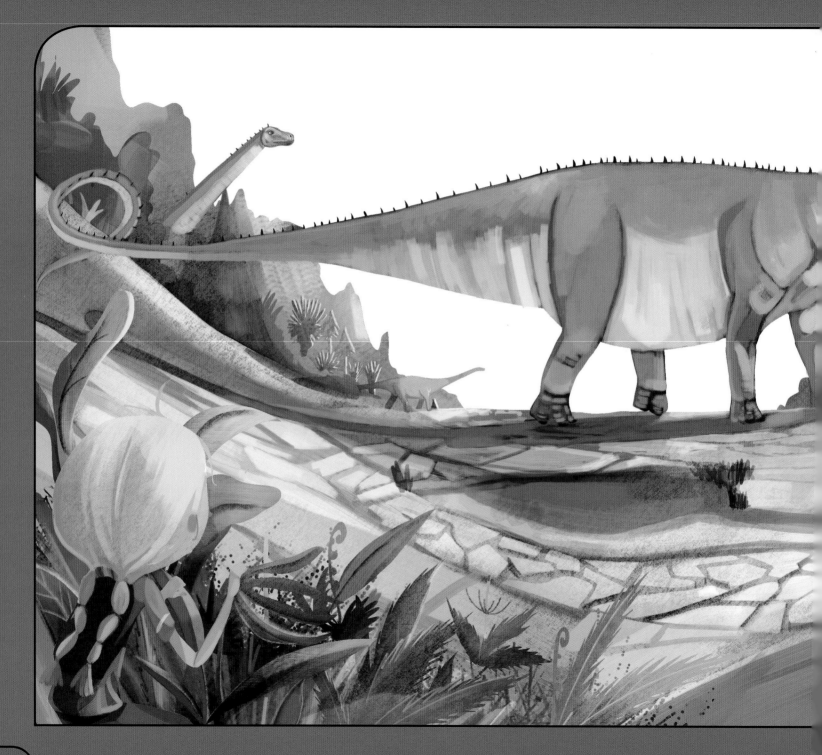

You found them! They're huge. One is 90 feet (27 m) long, nearly as long as a basketball court. It weighs more than three hippopotamuses, or 13 tons (11,793 kg). It would weigh more, but some of its bones are filled with air.

Get closer for a better view. See the spikes on its back? They're not bony. They're more like fingernails. They line the back of Diplodocus, from its head to its tail.

What did you find? A Diplodocus tooth! Cool, but not rare. Every 35 days, a Diplodocus gets a new tooth. Their teeth wear down quickly. Come see why.

Watch how Diplodocus eats. It bites down and then pulls the branch through its mouth. Its teeth strip off the leaves. That's hard on teeth!

Diplodocus can stand up on its two back legs. Its tail keeps it steady.

It strips leaves at the top of the tree.

You're thirsty. Take a swig. The Diplodocus herd is thirsty, too. They need water and more plants to eat. They head out of the forest. One Diplodocus moves very slowly. It is weak. But you better stick with the rest of the group.

The herd moves across the plain. Something rushes toward the Diplodocus that falls behind. An Allosaurus!

A healthy adult Diplodocus is too big for it to attack. But this weak one is easy prey. The herd must leave this Diplodocus behind.

You've come to a new forest. The river here has more water. A Diplodocus dips its head for a drink. Its nose is high on its head, so it can breathe while its mouth is in the water.

The herd eats and drinks. But your water is gone. You are hungry. Say goodbye to the herd. Time to head home.

WHERE HAVE DIPLODOCUS FOSSILS BEEN FOUND?

GLOSSARY

Allosaurus—A meat-eating dinosaur that lived at the same time as Diplodocus.

dry season—The time of the year, in certain climates, where very little rain falls.

extinct—No longer found living anywhere in the world; known only from fossils.

fossil—A bone or other trace of an animal from millions of years ago, preserved as rock.

herd—A group of animals that feed and travel together.

Jurassic Period—The time period from 200 million to 145.5 million years ago, when Diplodocus and other dinosaurs lived.

plain—A large, flat area of land, usually covered in grass.

prey—An animal that is eaten by another animal.

thicket—A thick growth of plants, bushes, or small trees.

AUTHOR'S NOTE

Too bad for us, time machines aren't real. But all of the details about Diplodocus in this book are based on research by scientists who study fossils. For example in 1990, a researcher noticed some rocks had impressions left by Diplodocus skin. That's how scientists discovered that Diplodocus had spikes! New dinosaur discoveries are made every year. Look up the books and websites below to learn more.

READ MORE

Allatson, Amy. *Diplodocus (All About Dinosaurs)*. New York: Kidhaven, 2017.

Hansen, Grace. *Diplodocus (Dinosaurs)*. Edina, Minn.: Abdo Kids, 2018.

Hirsch, Rebecca E. *Diplodocus*. Lake Elmo, Minn: Focus Readers, 2018.

Levine, Sara C. *Fossil by Fossil: Comparing Dinosaur Bones*. Minneapolis: Millbrook, 2018.

WEBSITES

DINOSAURS: EXTINCT BUT POWERFUL CREATURES—NATIONAL GEOGRAPHIC KIDS
http://kids.nationalgeographic.com/explore/nature/dinosaurs/
Compare sizes of dinosaurs, meet paleontologists, and more.

PBS KIDS: DINOSAUR GAMES
https://pbskids.org/games/dinosaur/
Play games, watch videos, and try online activities to learn more about these fascinating extinct animals.

Every effort has been made to ensure that these websites are appropriate for children. However, because of the nature of the Internet, it is impossible to guarantee that these sites will remain active indefinitely or that their contents will not be altered.